What Would The World Be Without Black People?

A Children's Book About Black History

Written & Illustrated By:
Erica M. Burrell M.Ed.

Copyright©2020 Erica M. Burrell

All rights reserved. No part of this publication may be reproduced, distributed, or transmitted in any form or by any means, including photocopying, recording, or other electronic or mechanical methods, without the prior written permission of the publisher, except in the case of brief quotations embodied in critical reviews and certain other noncommercial uses permitted by copyright law.

ISBN: 978-0-578-64779-1
Author: Erica M. Burrell
Illustrator: Erica M. Burrell

Published by: Published Power
www.PublishedPower.com

Published Power titles may be purchased in bulk for educational, business, or sales promotion. For information including ebook licenses please email info@publishedpower.com

Addison Grace, I love you daughter.

Dedication

This book is dedicated to every student I have ever worked with. You are capable of greatness and I truly believe in y'all.

Mrs. Burrell ♡

Timothy walked into class angry. Mrs. Burrell looked at Timothy and asked, "Timothy, why are you upset?" "Latifa took too long and I didn't get to swing today. I hate Black people and wish they were never born!"

" Hate?" Mrs. Burrell looked at Timothy disappointed. "You do know I'm Black, right? Do you hate me?" Timothy responded, "Well most Black people," he said under his breath. "Why do we need them anyway?" "Well, Timothy," Mrs. Burrell said, "I am glad you asked. Let's take a look at what your life would be like without Black people."

"Starting tomorrow, you will wake up and your life will look different. You will get your wish to live in a world with no Black people." Timothy left that Friday afternoon excited. "Good. My life will be much better without those people."

Timothy went home and finished his evening as usual: a bath, quick dinner, video games, and sleep. He went to sleep excited to wake up to no Black people ever existing.

Timothy woke up the next morning ready to get his day started. He turned on his iPod to play his favorite rapper, Tupac. He kept pushing play and nothing came on. The Knowledge Fairy flew into Timothy's room and said, "Tupac is a Black man Timothy. You're in a world with no Black people, remember?"

"Well then why are you here?" Timothy asked angrily. "I am not a Black person. I am a Black fairy, a magical Black fairy. My name is Knowledge Fairy, and everytime that you go to interact with something related to Black people, I will make sure you are unable to."

Not only was there no Tupac, Jay-Z, Missy Elliott, and other artists he loved, there was no hip-hop or rap music at all. "DJ Kool Herc, a Black man, was responsible for the hip-hop evolution you love today," said Knowledge Fairy with a smile.

DJ KOOL HERC

"I don't care," Timothy shrugged. "I'll just listen to something else." As he went to different genres in his iPod, everything was gone.

"Timothy," Knowledge Fairy continued, "Rock 'n' Roll began with Chuck Berry, a Black man in 1955, and Cab Calloway was one of the first R&B artists in the 1940s."

"Just so you know, Reggae and Pop music-" "OKAY Fairy," Timothy interrupted. "I get it, I basically can't listen to any of the music I like."

Knowledge Fairy popped up and said, "Tim, you're going to have to scrub the floor on your hands and knees. The mop was invented by a Black man named Thomas W. Stewart in 1893."

T. W. STEWART
WET MOP 1893

Frustrated, Timothy scrubbed the floors and got dressed. When it was time for him to put on his shoes, he noticed his shoe rack was empty. "Awww man," Timothy said annoyed. "I only had Jordan sneakers and those were made by a Black man too." Timothy put on his dad's shoes which were too big and asked his dad for a ride to the mall.

RICHARD SPIKES

"Ohhhhhh Timothy!" Knowledge Fairy sang as she flew into the room. "Your dad owns an automatic car. The automatic gear shift was created by a Black man named Richard Spikes in 1932. But, uh, nice shoes," Knowledge Fairy teased.

GARRET A. MORGAN

"Well, I'll just take the bus." "Not quite hunny," Knowledge Fairy replied. "The bus also uses a gear shift. Plus, it would not be safe because the Black inventor Garret Morgan is responsible for the contributions that made the traffic light we know today. You're gonna have to walk."

Timothy walked 30 blocks to the mall with no music. He started to realize life without Black people felt empty and cruel. When Timothy finally got to the mall he didn't see the usual elevator.

Up popped the fairy who said, " I think you have to take the stairs." Timothy looked at the fairy in disbelief. "Alexander Miles in 1887 created the automatic opening doors we use for our elevators and he was Black." "The game store is on the 22nd floor," Timothy whined. "Well you better start walking."

Timothy was so exhausted he decided to stop on the 12th floor for a hotdog and realized most of the food court was empty. "Hey, where is all the food?" Timothy asked out loud.

FREDRICK MICKINLEY JONES

"Most food delivery comes from a refrigerated truck. That was invented by Fredrick McKinley Jones – another Black man – around 1938. Would you like a bottle of water?"

Timothy sat down and drank his water before continuing up the stairs to the game store. When he finally arrived, he only saw one friend. "Hey Jeff, where is Paul, Tyrell, and Lauren?" Jeff looked at Timothy confused. "Who?" questioned Jeff.

Knowledge Fairy sprinkled her dust and chimed, "Timothy those other friends of yours were all Black. So you can't see them anymore." Timothy was overwhelmed with sadness. "What have I done?" he asked himself.

PHILLIP B. DOWNING
MODERN LETTER BOX

He continued wandering around the store looking for a video game. The one he wanted was sold out. He started to ask the cashier to order the game but then heard the fairy whisper, "Actually, he can't order it for you. A Black man named Phillip B. Downing invented the modern day mailbox in 1891."

Timothy walked the 30 blocks back home and thought about all the things he loved; cool dances, television shows, foods, clothes, and music. There were so many elements of Black culture that he took for granted. Timothy got home and noticed everything was destroyed. He asked a police officer, "What happened to our house?"

Before the officer could respond, Knowledge Fairy flew over Timothy and stated, "Osbourn Dorsey, a Black man, invented the doorknob in 1878 and Marie Van Brittan Brown, a Black woman, invented the first home security system in 1966. I am afraid because you could not use those inventions your home was robbed."

Having no bed because of the robbery, Timothy slept on the floor that night and decided not to do anything until Monday morning.

He ran into school Monday yelling, "Mrs. Burrell! I know you're Black, please come back, I'm sorry, I'm so sorry." Mrs. Burrell appeared in her bright yellow dress.

She looked at Timothy and said, "You know, everything about who you are would be different if it weren't for the contributions of Black people. Everybody who has a body is somebody, Timothy. I hope you learned a valuable lesson."

Mrs. Burrell turned to the class and said "Okay scholars, get out your notebooks".

Writer

Lena Waithe is a screenwriter, producer, and actress. She made history as the first Black woman to win the primetime Emmy award for outstanding writing for a comedy series in 2017. Waithe is also dedicated to mentoring writers of color.

Doctor & Inventor

Dr. Patricia Bath (1942-2019) invented the Laserphaco Probe, a tool that corrects cataracts during eye surgery. In 1988, Bath became the first Black female doctor to secure a medical patent.

Inventor

Madame C.J. Walker (1867-1919) invented hair care products for Black women. Walker became one of America's first self-made female millionaires in 1913.

Strategist

Symone D. Sanders is a political strategist, author, and former presidential press secretary. Additionally, she serves as a senior advisor for a presidential campaign & advocates for juvenile justice.

Mathematician

Born in 1918, Katherine Johnson is a mathematician whose calculations contributed to the U.S. having their first successful trip to space. She is one of few black women to work as an aerospace technologist at NASA.

Film Director

Ava Duvernay is a writer, director, producer and film distributor. She has directed movies and TV shows for companies like Disney. Amongst many accomplishments, to date, Duvernay is the highest paid Black woman director in American history.

Rapper

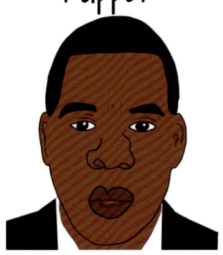

Shawn "Jay-Z" Carter is a self-made American billionaire who made his fortune as a rapper, producer, and investor. Additionally, he started the Shawn Carter Foundation, which is a non-profit that pays for students to go to college.

Producer

Missy Elilott is a songwriter, singer, dancer, and producer. In addition to having multiple platinum albums and Grammy awards, she is heavily involved in stopping domestic violence and has donated her time and resources to domestic violence awareness.

DJ

Clive "DJ Kool Herc" Campbell, known as the Godfather of hip-hop, is an American/Jamaican DJ who is credited with starting hip-hop music in the Bronx in the 1970s. His musical contributions have inspired many artists we listen to today.

Guitarist

Chuck Berry (1926-2017), known as the father of Rock 'n' Roll, was a singer and songwriter who evolved Rock 'n' Roll. He has opened the doors for many Black musicians today and his music still influences many up and coming artists.

Inventor

Marie Van Brittan Brown (1922-1999) was a Black woman who invented the home security system in 1966 in Jamaica, New York along with her husband Robert L. Brown. In addition to being awarded the patent for her home security system, Marie was also a licensed nurse.

Singer

Cab Calloway (1907-1994) was a jazz singer, dancer, and bandleader. He was the first African American to sell one million records from one song. His art influenced people like Michael and Janet Jackson.

Inventors

• Alexander Miles whose birthdate is unknown, was an African American inventor who held the US patent for the automatic opening and closing elevator doors in 1887.

Fredrick McKinley Jones (1893-1961) was an inventor and entrepreneur. He was inducted into the National Inventors hall of fame. He is best known for his truck refrigeration invention which helped keep food fresh while traveling long distances.

Osbourn Dorsey whose birthdate cannot be confirmed was an African American man likely born into slavery. He is credited with inventing the doorknob and door stopper in 1878 in Washington, D.C.

• Thomas W. Stewart (1823-1890) is an African American inventor who submitted his patent for the traditional mop on June 13, 1893 in Detroit, Michigan. This was major especially because slavery had just legally ended for Black people a few years prior in 1865.

• Phillip B. Downing (1857-1934) is an inventor who was responsible for the modern day mailbox we use today. Downing submitted his patent for approval in 1891 in Boston, Massachusetts.

• Richard Bowie Spikes (1878-1963) held many US patents including automobile directional signals, the automatic gear shift, and a braking safety system for trucks and busses. His contributions make our cars safer and more efficient.

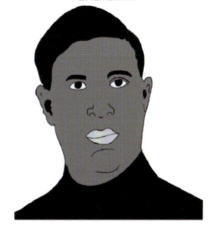

Garret A. Morgan (1877-1963) was an American businessman, inventor, and political leader. He invented the 3 position traffic light. In addition, Morgan donated to Black colleges and opened an all-Black country club.

• Due to a lack of documentation, little is known about some inventors. Dates are estimated, all inventions were verified through the United States Patent Office.